The Kit Poems

JAN-MITCHELL SHERRILL

The Stonewall Series
a division of
BrickHouse Books, Inc.
306 Suffolk Road
Baltimore, Maryland

ISBN: 0-932616-83-6

The bird would cease and be as other birds
but that he knows in singing not to sing.
The question that he frames in all but words
is what to make of a diminished thing.
                      - Robert Frost, "The Oven Bird"

Yes, I can be cruel. I have been taught by masters.
                      - Catherine Sloper, "The Heiress"

Acknowledgments:

My thanks to those who knew the truth of it all without once asking: Clarinda Harriss, Tara Woolfson and George Pereira, Michael and Robin Gieseke, Jason Schwartz, Jay Riskind, Seth and Kristy Weinshel, Michael Walker, Melissa Sherrill, Ginny Merryman, Anne Modarressi, Dan and Daisy Jones, Tony Frye and Rob Lischinsky, Richard Gorelick, and Sydney Gingrow. Special thanks to Bill and Linda Hazlehurst who offered me a home, and my deepest appreciation to Jay Jones, a national treasure, who is my right hand.

My gratitude to David Parker for a thorough reading; thanks to Chip Bouchard and Stephen Smith who made vital editing suggestions.

Cover by Tony Frye
Layout by Jay Jones

*For my sister, Melissa,
who knows more about
love and forgiveness than
anyone on earth;*

*and for the man whom
I trusted to be my
best friend, but was not.*

Contents

Introduction

I have long known that any new poem by Jan Sherrill will deliver the gist of lucid speech and a core of truth wrung from deep feelings. I should not be surprised, then, by *The Kit Poems*. But I am, by the many traits that were in part present or latent in his earlier work now here perfected.

The most surprising development is that he has moved from direct speech, so much prized by the past century's poets, to song, song like Lieder slipped free from fixed form. These are poems that must not be read by the eye alone. They demand to uncoil from the throat, curl over the tongue, sputter briskly with sharp sounds, or brood and gather doom with dark vowels, liquids, and glides. And the range of song is broad. "Violet" moves forward on pure melody; "Martin Luther Argues for Dancing" builds sophisticated syncopation; "The Complexities of Delray Beach" captures incantation. It is no small feat to bring song back to plain speech, as these poems do, especially heart and bone song: what's left when the body has embraced each of its passions then stepped back from them. Sherrill's lyric achievement alone warrants a permanent place for *The Kit Poems* in the collection of anyone who cares about the future of lyric poetry.

I also delight in how this new collection puts to work the horde of Sherrill's learning: the Bible, Renaissance drama, English lyric poets, British and American novelists, modern poets, ancient and an assortment of other histories, popular culture. Reading along, I find myself suddenly in a dialogue with Yeats, or Eliot, James, Marlowe, Auden, Frost, Donne, Shakespeare. Neither finial nor fretwork, as allusions so often are, each of Sherrill's dialogues with other writers is integral to the poems' structure, as well as a sharp insight into its source. At other times, he gives a different, new life to Biblical and historical persons long familiar and a little shopworn, a life rich with cunning understanding, as in "Emily Dickinson and Genghis Khan" or "David."

Finally, I note both the stunning metaphor with which Sherrill makes the familiar strange and fresh again and the clarity of his vision as he images a world for us. Consider the startling witness of the "lithe shoots of tulip, like tickly/ tongues of gossipy doubt through tepid mud" and the immutable presence of "Under the scarf, when it slipped,/ her skin was clay-molded, flood silt,/ mounds from nothing, unmoving the way/ something affixed does not move." These are not clever observations. Rather, they are the kind that only come through wisdom, and they generously impart that wisdom. And, like Mrs. Dalloway's "I give it to you," it is lovely and can't be undone.

"Teaching one's self is like stopping blood/ flow," Sherrill says in "Change, Again." I don't believe him for a moment. A poem like "Carnival," tells us what his self has learned, and it makes the blood race, the mind race. *The Kit Poems* unflinchingly gives us Sherrill's learned self, a solid gift, one that will serve, like a fine tool or a perfect object, to be taken up and used or cherished again and again.

Dan Jones
President Emeritus
and Professor of English
Towson University

Emily Dickinson and Genghis Khan

for Anne Modarressi

I am not certain, but we may
have met. In a pause from slaughter,
you stopped to stare: a small,
red wren, dressed white as narcissus,
in the midst of the horses and blood. We
spoke, I think, about the endless
steppes; how you ride them, low
to the bitter grass, how you dream
of flying over the meadow in Chinese bloom.
I told you about my room in Amherst
and my mother's death, that I
watched the light leave her face
like a trimmed wick; unlike your swift
dispatch, she went in inches.

Then, your eyes left my face. The long
light faded flat. In moments we were as drawn
thought, then dimmer, then gone.

Dorothy Parker Complains in Heaven

The gin doesn't burn going down. Dog shit
disappears by itself. And nobody cares a whit
about my cussing or that I never write.

I'm the only white one here, so
there is a God, the broken, slow-
witted son of a bitch, is only an echo
of me. Not Hell. They told me right away:
there isn't one. Above the world is
a residential hotel. A good business
in widows who stumble down its corridors
when they're drunk. Where is Hemingway, that prick?
Even he dies; he deserves eternal happiness,
and the end of the world was always in his eyes.

The Lindbergh Baby

Too young to be afraid of death,
falling, confinement to sleep, these
were my dark shapes. When I died,
it was balloon burst, ballast gone,
I floated up. Not the crying, screaming
black headlines could tether me.
I combined: chill with sea fog,
rain with salted fish—all sky.
I fly over Bethlehem as the innocents die;
Farmington, Connecticut, its brutal Christmas,
a whole child used to define adulthood:
loss they think of when they think
of unutterable loss. I catch the milk
carton faces, fervent prayers, perverse
desires. In my picture face there are
parameters: comfort in the two, small sightless
eyes. Now I am night and air.
I buoy my father's plane, high into the glare
of sunlight, up, up all the way
to limitless dark. We meet there.

He says, "Release me." He, as he was,
floats, too: before sorrow, his need for worth,
love; the will to define us deflates
us and drops him, no longer endless,
back to earth. Father, my dearest
unforgiven father, if you love, let it go,
though it scares you, I know, please do;
I will pour down all over you.

Beauty Burns

Under the scarf, when it slipped,
her skin was clay-modeled, flood silt,
mounds from nothing, unmoving the way
something affixed does not move. Clarinda,
by me, quickly took my hand, her smooth
athletic skin, taut over my own
cold, frozen fingers. As she talked
to us from across her desk,
I kept charted on her gorgeous
face, perfect make-up, sunny hair. Beneath
her scarf, the coils of unliving skin
told us what beauty had been: life
returns a kitchen fire, smoking in bed,
negligee in silken flames. An ash
falls; she turns away. Beauty
is in all of us, and it burns.

Birches on US 91

Living in birches, not breaking,
though thin white arms of love
seem so fragile, deceive me
with white shadow teeth gleaming.
Their rapacious hunger sighs,
they bend, speak of risk that
quells with sway. Supplicants
to all that weighs down, forces up—
no end of waving an "all-clear"
to we on cracking knees.

They are
climbing tigers, albino stripes,
mate and mateless in variegated light.
I ride them, swinging high,
a speaking winter over the charcoal
lines of US 91, tender tall things
that hold forever, their bleaching
branches in peerless night.
Lost amidst them, and found among them.
I could do worse. I could go first.
Into blinding day, in plain sight.

Blanche DuBois and Her Son

Who does he look like? Do his bangs
fall onto his forehead with an intensity
of light, shining hair that Moonlake
only imitates? It is hard to see his
face tonight; it is sheltered by the half
wing of his mother's sleeve, for her arm
encircles him: they are dancing.

The "Tennessee Waltz" played by a cello
lifts them, dust-light, around the floor.
He looks like his dead father, the gay
boy whose gray, folded letters—serenades
from a suicide—she still keeps. He
never knew she was pregnant, never
knew how his shredded life might define
her, even now, as she glides their little
boy, anesthetized and wholly delivered
by the glamour of her pain, this night
and the even grace of a sad old waltz,
circling them—as they turn—the only
couple on earth, around and around
the empty dance floor.

David

What I knew about them all
was they could convince themselves
of anything. Goliath leaned into his fall
and gave me his head, willingly. Saul
believed God chose me, so I came
between them; and Jonathan, the easiest;
I let him think he loved me.

God did speak to me. In my lonely
reverie He came, more silent than a
wolf, subtle as the dissonance in minor
chords. He the Lord of yellow eyes
blinking through dark mountain skies,
gave me the promise of victimhood. Once
His, He shot the stone between the giant's
eyes, made Saul doubt every part of himself,
and led me straight to Jonathan's heart.

Eternity is this way, father against son,
coercion, intimidation that comes from
recognizing love is neither real nor unreal.
We do to others what we make of ourselves:
Saul, the unwanted; Jonathan, the lover; David,
the King. I played victim while I wore
his ring, and he wished for more from me.
The ashy mouth of fire speech, love that spans
the breach of time. He wanted songs
that sang my depth of feeling for him.
Victim upon victim, longing for a psalm
to ignite some final vision, compensatory
sight of the sensuous made sensible, when
truth is only God's left eye; His right
never opens to reveal the sheer

plunge of longest night. Jonathan's heart
was not full, but swollen from the sting
of my dear arrow. He coerced me
into love; I let him. I killed him;
he let me, and God's predatory world
moves on, a cocking gun. How
are the mighty fallen.

Diaghilev Has His Say

The little monkey danced me blind.
Into white rages I followed him
as I thought Christ would have
sought His missing lamb. I
recovered him from mocking
peasants who knew only
crickets hopped so high. He
got strong. I was jealous
of every board his twisted feet
flew from, and he grew
to love me in that way
only artists know: obsession,
worn like a ring his thumb
spun and spun in ever-tightening
sights of an ever-aiming gun. He
was always pointed at me.

I don't care what others see;
or if I am wrong. Universal
love is the vapid thing of saints
gone to rack, buried by stones.
Sacrifice, forsaking all others,
made him dance. Error, loneliness,
silence like a dial tone, the heart,
unanswered—these are bred in our bones.
I made Nijinsky love me and me alone.
He moved free among the wolves then,
lifted the world like a ball
on the points of his flashing knees.
It was selfish of me to save
him, protect him, bind him to me?
His madness came: fat; that
badly dressed Buenos Aires woman

her savage hat of pinned bird wings.
Suffering was a narrow light,
the corridor dark, and soft—his heart,
free, away from me.

Elijah and the Widow

"And she said unto Elijah, what have I to do with thee. O thou man of God? Art thou come unto me to call my sin to remembrance, and to slay my son?"
                                        -- 1 Kings 17:18-19

I don't know where he came from or how
he got to me. We fed him from a
jar of meal, which filled each night
while we slept. He had been fed
by many things: he told me ravens
brought him meat and bread before
he came to me. He is one of those
sustained by food I cannot see.

After a year of living with us, my boy
and me, I found my only son lying
naked on the floor—what was my
sin that his cold god should kill
my child? He was dying; I watched
it spread, a fist of confused contagion
pounding him empty as a hole: dead.

Then I don't know what I saw. Elijah
picked the dead boy up and carried him
to his own room. I followed there,
where he laid him on his bed and affixed
himself, palm to palm, belly to belly: mixed
themselves in front of me. Was death
so intimate? It looked like what my
husband did to me. Then, my son shuddered.
Elijah rolled onto his back, spent.
What had I seen? Freed from tomb, my boy
bounded away, and the prophet lay
in the fading light of his bedroom.

Late Bloomer

For Tara Woolfson

My parents never said I was ugly,
but they dressed me in ways that covered
me up. Had veils been worn in those days,
I would have been draped in yards of voile,
a small statue never destined for display.

The years of yearning began. I fell
in love so easily—plain boys, whose eyes
were full of forgetfulness, hands never in motion:
those I loved in ways that sex was merely cold
approximation; I thought they were deep; deeply blind.

St. John said hope would be hope for the wrong thing,
so I shuddered in my bed, pretended I was
dead after syncopated touching. When Beauty said,
"I love you," to the Beast, his ugliness melted like the first
snowfall. But they perceived no change in me.

Out front, where the big girls stand, there is nothing
deeper than paint. I am the secret of veneer, the ring
that turns your finger green. This year I may wait
for you—who knows—my eyelashes may grow and you
might see some inner glory. It will
not be beauty. I was never in that story.

Martin Luther Argues for Dancing

I can dance. It was hard
to trust my feet—they were
so used to Earth, I had
to leave them completely
behind. At first, I was
a deer haunch spinning
on sticks. Then I learned:
it was will before belief.
That led me to total abandon,
and I whirled, coarse wool
flying, my skinny legs rubbing
a firestorm. All the crickets
in the county answered my louder
mating call. Do not be cowed
by how foolish you look: I
do it gracelessly, crookedly,
and I pant. There is so much
sorrow, you must dance, fall
into fits, break your hip, twist
as though pain can be shaken
from your limbs; fingertips,
kneecaps, spigots gurgling
bile and anger out the pink
reservoir of you. Devil is
the quiet weep, the lonely
cinder make-up, the sausage-
tied gut of solitary thought.
Jesus is your partner, purple
tiger striped with untapped
veins of wiggling blue. Tame
and teach Him, too. I promise:
hours will cohere in deep surrender.
It is night; the Glory has shut up—
without red sun and a black
moon rising, you sleep.
You finally sleep.

My Stalker's Picture

For RSB

It came in an unmarked envelope,
postmarked New York City. Such
anonymity for so singular a gift.
An old photograph, a snapshot really,
of him at 16—it was written on
the back. I flipped it over and
over, only taking in the image
in small increments—hair,
he had it; eyes, blue and
unreflective, azure marble
like Caribbean water, clear
to the depth of socket.
His straight nose, full lips,
parted to show the orthodonture,
his wholly forbidding mouth. Below
he is naked, with erection,
and the golden squeals of teen-
aged girls, though unseen, trumpet
from the picture. In black
pen he has printed my name
on the constant shaft of his penis.

With razor blade I extract
the febrile shape, his dick,
my name to fit a dime-sized locket.
Around my neck, he will wander
as I move; he swings, a guillotine
of hate and monstrous devotion.
On the coldest day next year I will
throw it into the ocean off the Provincetown
pier: dead treasure for greedy seekers
of vanished life, killing weather.

Nureyev in the Atlanta Airport

He was a motionless figure.
Not tall; what height he had
was stored in his floor-length
sable that was flung around him,
sphinx shawl, Balzac pose. Unlikely,
but he turned his head slightly to watch
me pass: he, the dying Olympian,
I, a fat man with bags. Alike
in desire, his hauteur made us bound
to ignore the improbability
of rapture. I think he wanted
nothing, someone who did not
scream, "More!" I was eager
to score the man whose leap
through the air was ending at ground.
The human traffic rushed
'round us; the Russian,
at the bottom of the falling world—
peasant more than grace, fear—
the roar of jet engines' carnal
lullaby, buzzing in our ears.

Prayer for the Ordinary

Oh God, make him ordinary—
someone I can't build or amplify;
no muse, no man whose heart
speaks at all. Let him be single-
minded—I am all he wants
for what I merely appear to be.

There is no depth in me left
to fathom. I sail, banners furled:
we will lie, close together, at
the bottom of the flooded world.

Let it mean only what
it is, or nothing. Stop me
from thinking, wanting, even
blinking once to clear my eyes.
I will give up light, feeling wonder;
deny all I know to have been true.

Or, tell me he comes bringing
you with him into my room;
I will prepare his way:
where he walks, candles dance, his shoes
the flames that lift for life resumed:
I am yours. Let my cry come echoing to you.

Skin

It won't come off by any means
available: No kingly flailing,
no monkish flagellation
to remind me what lives below.
I know: it shows all over me,
dries, flakes, scabs, tells
what else I am.
                I could live happy.
Insect skeleton face to meet
the world. A pearled
sheen of tapping joy; nothing
to pinch or bruise, blunder or use
a dry canvas for some
rigor smile. I could not cry, lie
easily, or see an aging face that
yelps its recognition in
my morning mirror.
Beetle smooth, moth soft.
I am inside out, itching for
permanent detachment from
all things that hang blue and
subtle just inside me. It
could all be outside me;
look like no one, wear nothing.
Goodbye to the stinging, the singing,
every indifferent caress.
On a breeze, I would be gone.

Speaking for the Dead

for Jay Jones

I dream of a love so selfless,
I will not matter. Dead
friends are not easy,
for they pull me back to them,
in body where I touched,
in mind where I thought
I loved them. I
must be somewhere
where I am not. An end
of eye, a limit of hand;
I must slip past feeling
to flat expanse—shoulders,
a desert; jaw, sheer
mountain, dropping off
to immeasurable snow.
When I go, I will not come
back; do not look for me:
there will be idle
remorse, then singing,
then nothing heading North,
North, North to nothing at last.
Hear me, it will be air
rushing past. Love will
be mastless sailing, a bird,
a car careening in the failing pink,
iodine light of a forgotten
and wholly invented day.

Violet

She occupies only the side of her bed.
Her body an edge to the gilded frame,
shape beneath the scarlet spread,
the 600-count Egyptian cotton sheets.
She, this skeleton Pasha, so regal
in reverse; the room is golden,
and the Chippendale chest is amber
in her dying, deposited light.
Night passes through her on foxfeet.
I meet her eyes, clouded with Klonopin
and Demerol. She sits up—the linen
is at attention, and the half moon
rising at her window, spills cream
across her white, hanging gown.

The bruises, like clematis, climb
her arms. She smiles at nothing.
I am the clock she counts by.
I play Doris Day. "Gonna take
a sentimental journey..." as she
sways almost unnoticed. Far away,
my father is taking her hand. She steps
down to the bedroom floor. And,
as she taught me 40 years ago,
we bebop slow before my father's
ghost hand lets her drop
behind the bandstand. I lift her
back into bed; her thumb corrects
my eyebrows. Blood tomorrow,
open veins, shelved vials. Relentless
life long tasks. "Am I wearing my
pearls? Where are my dancing slippers?"
She always asks.

Spring Defies Me

For Richard Wilbur

Two fat bees, so stunned
by weight and lust, they,
in utter fervor, fuck three
inches above the ground,
their black, leaden buzzing
to annihilate death. Everything
blessed is probing for the wet,
sticky wonder that will free
them. It is apparent: this
all goes on forever. Baby bottle
floating in the Tidal Basin
under howling cherry blossoms—
and the sun—is it someone's last
or a first that means nothing
to a gurgling brain? My shoes
are petal-stained, my throat
closes with yellow dew.

Rub me, my love, 'til the white
pasty skin shows through again.
I want November back, with
endings so complex: spring
forgotten with its ragged
thrusts of reptile robins.

Steel Pier Diving Horse

For Dan Jones

We waited in line to see the horse
and diver leap, 50 feet above the Boardwalk,
into the small tub of water. Lifted to the
scaffold, dressed in flaming silks, connected
by only tenuous reins, they paused,
then flew, pop lights exploding, toward
the fragile little pool, rickety,
tinseled with seashells and a
mermaid of nylon gold hair.

Over and over in memory they plunge.
Will they die, swept into each other,
the yellow circle of carnival lights
their only Milky Way? Gliding through
air each remembers a riderless horse,
a man of wishbone contortion, longing,
pitched like a horseshoe into open air.

Does the rider stroke the withers that
have held him so long, to calm the horse
at death? Does the horse, in shiver to acknowledge
the wondrous touch, vibrate, "You are safe
with me; hold to me: we go straight
together, wet weight, into vaporous nothing."

Without a net, which one loves, which
is lover, friends of steep fall and shatter?
They are laddered to each other in reflected fear,
reassurance. Does one hold the other? Who
gives himself wholly? In their precipitous fall,
each gives to the other, the narrowing life of care,

the unreasoned, artless, harrowing care.
As they plummet, will they know the nature
of their love, for they fall.

I will stop talking now. Listen
to the horse, his rider, for the stilled
cacophony, whispered sound, a trove
of nuance and assemblage: fearless,
ex parte, remembered matrimony:
what we don't know beyond their memory,
understanding—the surety of our
doubt, and how well they know love.

Sylvia Plath Explains Art to Me

For Sharon Bahus

Remember what Blake said, "Rose, thou art
sick." It's not a question, you see.
Beauty is the thing that curls inward finally.
Red is not it. You are the rose.
Your husband is the beauty. Mine was. He's
the gorgeous greed that makes you
want him. Finally, burrowed in your
stupid heart, his black hair edges
every petal and—you're sick.
The trick was to write it all down. Can
you write it? I couldn't speak to him;
could barely speak at all.
The hallway of our house held
his car coat left behind. I went
blind one night when I saw it
there. But I wrote, recovered
sight and melted him forever
in the sliding waxed floors
in the polished dinette I wrote on
night after night until he was
really gone. Did he love me? Yes,
he did, and I thought I loved him,
right up until I cut him in half
and saw the biopsied beauty
like an inverse fish athrash
in my tea-stained sink.
Never think. Write it down:
rose thou art the dogs
of hell, yipping in my bath
tub, nails on attic boards, above
shivering sound in all directions.
He'll come home. I will paint
my toes. Red. He will call me
from my butchering: "Rose?"

Poem to Someone Once Named Donald Francis

Who are you? Some name evolving
away before I ever knew the specimen,
the small green piece, the bud connected nowhere.

I see you now, a man self-conscious
and angry at nothing he ever sees. Men
enrage him happily; he smiles an
edgy smile, moves away almost imperceptibly:
a rabbit-hole escape, ice fishing with a stun gun.
In the sun, alone, he is always radiant, shine like a stain.
I think it would be something to know you, plain:
the unregenerate, the unforgiving, the silent,
loving man no one can name.

Kit, Asleep on the Yellow Couch

"The visions all are fled…and in their stead
A sense of real things comes doubly strong,
And, like a muddy stream would bear along
My soul to nothingness, I will strive against
All doubt…"
                    -- John Keats, "Sleep and Poetry"

I couldn't shake off the enchantment:
your hands, those folded things that electrify
words, or unwind you completely when they stretch
above your head, were at rest,
delicate, with the even sound
you made sleeping on my couch.
I cannot follow you to that cool island, far
from all men's knowing. You have slipped,
someone else's guest, more secret than a nest
of nightingales. You sleep, and the world slows,
boundless now, a death of luxury: the thoughts
that make you are curled inside your head.
All you have said is sweeter now; you are stilled
motion, ardent mutterings, the thread
of you stitched, restitched, to cover your bed,
a growing shelter of softer fleece.
I am always so slow; you so hurried:
I feel safe while you sleep. Let the night worry
away. Your dreams are endless and touch
the edges of my moonlit start of day.

The Eraser

I found the eraser from your pencil;
it was what had so annoyed you earlier
when you dropped it. The figured rug,
too figured for sense, hid it. "Fuck!"
you said.
            When you'd gone, I was alone
in my yellow dining room, with the table we had
worked on, small ribs of our beginning
life, our headstones, our lake of floating
miracles: the scattered paper and books
were tender, age-worn as still stones we
step on toward each other, to cross a moving
brook.

Helpless in sudden emptiness, the emperor's
yellow was jaundiced without your serious face:
I saw the pencil eraser,
left like an egg beneath your chair.

And I rolled it in my hand, smooth
as your calm eye on mine: it is the wonder
of blood to bandage, the shelter
of rock to wing,
whatever catches any falling thing.

I had been angry that you were leaving
for Arizona, with my desert higher, me
in the driest of empty spaces.
                        Your eraser
in my hand was what I kept of you, like
a stupid teenager, through the weekend,
as you flew back and forth across America,
shape of your plane an X on every cloud,

and the shadow below on land, a cross, a set
of space, squares that touch, frame
each other, as our features touch our faces.
Through freakish, changing time, stale air,
over green, split, brown, thriving trees,
back, forever forward, to me.

Tonight I used the pencil and eraser
and drew your plane two
times on tracing paper. One long
winged thing with 40 holes for portals,
your face in every window of that plane;
then, the smallest dot of flying rage
so white, blank sky filled up the page.

As we bend the world to fit us, if we
string it as a harp, why can't I hear
distance as a note and not as loss?
Pictures, I draw pictures of you, smudging, tossing
everyone away until I learn your lines, their intersection
with mine. It is shadow, not shaping, blotting, not yet
blending color tones. Still, I love
the lines I make of you. Please come home.

Time

*"I do not fear the time. Who knows how my
love grows, who knows where the time goes?"
                    -- Judy Collins*

Big and round as a dinosaur's back,
this, whatever we name it, is solid. Brick
the size of Mars has come to rest, and I
conscientiously take its measure.
How do I cross it, straddle it? How
do I ride it without disappearing
into a forest of scales?
                              And you barely notice it
is in the room. But when you do, you say,
"Let's paint it white and leave it." Day
after day it soon becomes the wall left
unadorned, a gorgeous space: no over,
no under. "It is flying," you say.

It may be, for now, I only dream it.
And the romantic is the romance; beauty
has no surface: there is no literary
counterpart for us. Time is flame,
and it changes names in smoky, silken movement,
all of it the burnished glow of a cello
you learn to play, season after white season.

Waiting for Snow

Briefly, on Nov 24th, just before dawn,
it snowed in DC. You, far away
in Connecticut, emailed me that Dulles
had recorded an inch or so. "And you
will see the first snow fall this year without me."
It was raining when I woke to see.

Farmington was blanketed—a pure
white sheet that buried rattling speech,
silenced budding greed for each
other across the 700 miles of commuter
roads and tunnels that furrowed
families, connectors under Oz's
Emerald City. I have waited
patiently for it to come again. This
winter of disconsolate love
and closer, closer absence has
brought, instead, the kamikaze
blooms of forsythia—yellow screamers,
and lithe shoots of tulip, like tickly
tongues of gossipy doubt through tepid mud.
My blood would believe what my
heart has not: one good freeze
will stop this slide into all I
do not understand: freak weather
and promise of promise sworn
from distance, near, far.

Through blinding snow last night,
a bar in New Bedford, whaling village
of scarred men, was visited by
an axe-wielding man—Melville's
ghost so in love with Hawthorne,

he hacked up every gay man
in reach. Blood into the snowy
streets, arms of tender teaching
that held a lover's secrets, split
to the bone. Oil lamps became
circling klieg lights to search the storm.

The monster lurches away into
the snow. Red tracks leading past
the docks, the ancient whalers,
hoary white, stowed for nests
of crows and bitter gulls.
Tracks in snow: his—now mine—
in conflated time of TV news.
It snows on the maimed,
the terrorized, the terror itself.
Wait for snow; it brings silence,
absence, lies, death. It brings
focus on the love that defies methedrine,
on the beautiful, mangled bodies pitched
wildly; a flailed tattoo of my name, patch
of red, blue, red, red, red—stain
of controlled Kandinsky, or a cartoon
soul, like me, blackening night
against the unmoving, ever-burying white.

Lonesome Cowboys

A word from a cowboy song. In my
mind's eye, I see you sleeping
by campfire. The crest of surrounding
hills quietly wakes to steep glory,
and you open to the white face of snow
on the mountain. I imagine you there,
scent of hemlock and cedar in your hair.
You watch intently for two riders, watch
through snow for two figures who aren't there.

Back at sea level you are tired of feeling:
sadness you can't write through; the prettier
actor, wrongly cast in the film we see—
in your dream movie, he is your lover; alone
in the crowded theatre, you luxuriate
in your singularity of grief; I watch you,
only to know how your relief may come.

In the Wyoming snowstorm and horse bridle jangle,
the low viola plays that eternal note. If you
touch me, you feel it; watching you, I see it:
abides like music in heart beat, ebbs out life's
little day. Other people, most people never
have or do what they want; live out
separation, distortion, dead-letter piles,
false starts, unresolved partings; fragments
of promise crackle forever on short wave radios.

Listen to me: change is ours—give it to no one
else. I cannot quit you, break you, or flatten
to weather the storm of your grief, one that began
with a father, his arms full of gifts, too late,
turned away from that novocained Christmas:

decay, decay, decay. The world is tired
of waiting and bristles with each broken pairing.

Watch with me: two riders come
over the mountain, just there, above
the fault line. Wake, my love, be courageous:
grief is design in ice; we live twice,
another chance to smell the cedar, lie
again by the campfire in first, clean snow.
Take my hand. Let the rest argue, miss, and cry.
Let them go, dearest friend, riderless, into the
hungry sky.

Advent on G Street

Dec 9th, 2:30 in the morning, across
from the police station on G Street, you
have come from a bar where your straight
friend, as you leave, hugs you so tightly,
it is as if he will never let go. "I love you,"
he says. The glow of that serendipitous
embrace follows you now, his citrus cologne
still alive on your shirt; it starts to snow.
And high up, from an iPod or an old vinyl
record played by some lonely queen,
Thelma Houston sings, her thrumming
contralto, warm as indigo—in excelsis deo—
through the slow, purple morning.
                                        Christ is coming.
The angel-low voice that sang the Baths to ashes
is in the air, lush with expectancy, calm
with certainty of prophecy, destiny, birth. Christ
will come, soft as snow, new—the sudden friendship
of earth, sky. Your bed lies empty and you stand
outside; cold can't stop you, feeling at the end
of something, a list checked off—every item—wanting
to forget yourself—but how, when you've looked
so constantly for you? She sings: love calls
us to the things of this world. Carpenters,
truck drivers are born and reborn: turning
on a dishwasher in a broken house becomes
the expiation of that confused place; its lullaby
of flapping sound soothes the fearful to sleep.
She sings and bids us clear dances in the sight
of heaven. Time is chance and the great leavening.
Now you are loosed from cold planet. Is
the world still lit by lightning? The angel believes
you know. "Don't leave me this way," Gabriel

sings to the Virgin. Does he know: she will
not leave but will pass breathtakingly into
something else? Love calls her to the things
of this white world, the star winking like
a satellite, a rabbit backing into snowdrift,
the hiding wet eye of forever. Come
into the circle of light: glad tidings
for you, for Mary, salamanders in freezing
downspouts; cops, rats, and the wet
snow free of despair. Christ is coming;
he is in your sights. Contentment is yours
this whole and singular night.

Christmas Eve, Balto/Connecticut, 2005

No dead man's eyes to mar
the stars of Christmas Eve. Exiled
to my mother's porch to smoke, I know
the breathing stars amass above
Connecticut tonight.
                  What could unravel,
night tapestry of constant travel, will not;
the lilt of carols, whispered from Relay
Town Hall, quiets my guilt of missing you,
selfish amidst the clatter of giving.
Everything is living tonight.
                    Do they know
the savior of the night is in Connecticut,
know he dreams there of perfect phrase,
and subtle metaphor, hidden in the snow's
own moonlight, far away from me? His
eyes reflect Bethlehem, bright star; lead
the kings through restless search,
to surrender, to the nesting
nightingales of Farmington.

The hymns are finished, my cigarette
done; my mother creaks slowly up
the stairs to bed, shaking her head
at my smoking. No dead man
in the stars, rain for Christmas Day,
the first martyr's feast. I am so tired:
I sleep upon a mattress made
of grace, threaded with living fire.

Kit's Dream

Thunder, at its most awful, slips
under clouds, flaps through lightning,
skips storm completely and rests, gripping
you. Your ears are useless; this is deeper in,
as intimate as a stranger, housed in dream,
pecking at your eyes: he will hold your hand.

Are you lost in the fragrance of that bed? Madness
shoots, circular in the dark, and you, the weary
teacher of all immaculate, tethered feeling, let go
to drift in altitude—cousin to the rumble you only
half hear—take his hand to wander through your bedroom.

Tomorrow you will feel lonely: where is he,
what did it mean, leaving you so purely loved,
so cautiously held, so tenderly deaf, alone?

What have you shown me in a week:
my life, an indefinite line, crossed
at this moment in time. Speak—I am
waiting for the downpour, waiting closer
than either of us ever let in. The air thins, ozone
to ether, while you dream of love and surrender.

Portrait: Kit in Love

"And the room, where light strikes through the slits,
cherishes love, for here it is still new."
                    -- Anna Akhmatova, "Evening Room"

You said as you were walking in the bookstore
you knew you loved me. Apropos of nothing you
told me, quickly explaining there wasn't anything
about Barnes and Noble to prompt it. I suppose
you thought I may feel it to have been a literary love:
lost, old poetry, translated from the tougher, darker
expression.

So many loves, they beg us to choose:
whether Alexander spared Pindar's house
to flatter Aristotle; or the sort
that blessed Cleopatra's final love, her funeral dress
a small black snake. Love can requite you, and,
for your sake, the repeated aire of all sad poets
brings tower, house, apartment to the ground.

I cannot move as you tell me, your head down:
some shy thing, or a worry your eye will not convey
all it might say—less or more, smooth love
like ice—I cannot move. I feel it, too; berate
myself, knew as you said it so casually, you were
the wary change in everything, and everything was true.

I am living for the last time, not as molting bird,
nor shedding maple, no distant, dying star
swept into vapor. I hold our disparate thoughts
together, breathing in and out.
                              If we bought us at an
auction—a painting—how

unposed we would be: a portrait of two
men at a table; in its center would be
objects piled as treasure. Value is a secret thing between
us. How could someone see
our glittering eyes, so small is eyelight,
shining matchglow on the wing of a flea?
The painting: Theoxenia set for Pindar;
Yeats's worn moon shines above it; carved
along the table's apron, "Seigneur, ayez pitie de nous,"
as was written above Akhmatova's bed. For her, the
light meant love was new, its skeleton through shutter
slats mapped the way: and I would
pay all I have for this picture of us;
dance and lay down my head on its scripture.
Time comes; you knew it first: at this table is my seat.
At it, with you, for my calm, white end,
I will sit and eat.

Dying Alive

*"For what was this room but a place to forget we are
dying?"*
   -- Andrew Holleran, "Dancer From the Dance"

I think this is a room we die in.
Just you and I, in and out, imaginative,
lucid, then dense, surging at times with
turgid, tightening life.
                        I have come here to die;
for once I will make it right. To others I lie
about what I've felt, feel. Now I tie
what's left, this emblem of loss, sighs,
missed meanings, mounting trivialities
and lack of consequence to you; sheet woven, I die
in you, so final, it's as though sound
was never uttered. Spider could not move round
its fragile web, wings beat down, not skyward,
and everything we knew that ever flew
is bound, stilled, with us.
                        Why do we meet here, now?
You say destiny, but shy away from committing
belief. Lay your hands, your sleeping head, flat
upon your own arms; your leg still trembles:
blood at play, the need of muscle to believe.
I may never know how we found us; our souls are
sense, and so the world is bowed, unstrung.
We slide to its center; we hang on its spin,
narrow to wide.

I die to enter you—not ghost nor spirit
of sublunary intent. We collide by design, by
dream, by appetite, and what we do
together eats life. Wit is tender, sorrow

opaque as fish. We move as
underwater, light fighting to the top for our
sheltered, eyelash air.
        One day—long in you—our four eyes
stare out at endless night. Wet from the feel of you,
we are starlight now, and dew. Even as I tell
all this, the blue world ripens, full, eager to resume,
become true again. I am dying
alive in this room with you.

Meaning to Believe

*"Intreat me not to leave thee, or to return from following
after thee: For whither thou goest, I shall go; and where
thou lodgest, I will lodge: Thy people shall be my people,
and thy God, my God. Where thou diest, I will die and
there I will be buried."*
                    -- Ruth 2:16-17

I read the lines aloud: whom do I convince?
The simplicity of the statement is art to me:
I meant to believe. But who is this woman?
standing in the open flap of a tent, desert stretching all
around, she indentures herself—the compassion
and relief overwhelm me. I mean to believe her.

I am falling down a well to the bottom of me.
I drop away from the dime of light where your full life
plays out its sensual dance of forgiveness, hope; its
song after song of perfect pitch without me. You do
not entreat me; I am always free to go. Is that what
makes Ruth's plea so pure, my eyes glow when I read
it, crying because Naomi can't let her go? This is
Naomi's story, not Ruth's. It is she who can open the
eye of the tent, show the desert so empty and eager for
the narrow footprints leading away. Naomi, childless,
full of her God, decides Ruth's worth. Footprints
down the hollow well, yellow camel tracks circling,
circling Ruth's whole earth.

Kit's Windows

We began this way. Light on
or off from my apartment, he
said he watched. Though he
made schedules, kept calendars,
whole matrices of activity, the
lamps meant something else.
He was not Leander, he would
not drown on G Street.
The sky he maps rains
back on him always what
he feels, or feels no more.

I have watched for light
from him two times: New
Year's Day, home after
so long away. I slept
that night unencumbered
by the vision of snowy roads
and trucks that dragged his
Jeep in tow; then, last night,
when street lamps shone against
his closed white blinds in
city darkness; the moon, a
piece of melon rind, X-ray
glimmer of the ghost that
delivers hope: my mother
will never die, no lies, ever,
that we tell each other
or ourselves. The light
in his eye must not go out,
extinguish nothing in my own;
that I am home all night,
and he still watches. Our

windows, magnets that attract/
repel experience, the shell of
vapor that encases our
incandescence. Windows to
a moon forever rising, pulling
tides of human voices that
cannot drown. Watch for things
that surprise us from
behind, all around; for
phosphenes of sleepy blindness,
fragment light to amaze, confound.

Vladimir's River

It is the Miass River. A good one,
"full of fish." He pantomimes
casting, reeling in with a flick
of his fingers, the line, the catch.
In winter the ice is 80 feet thick;
tractors he designed drive from
the factory across that frozen road
to the transport fleet on the other side,
while skaters dart, ground minnows,
in and out the rolling line, through
the day long twilight. Candles
in hand, from the bridge where he
fishes in summer, it is all
a Disney creation of DNA clusters,
spinning their orbit in pure atom comfort.

"When we go to Russia, I will
fish for you and cook a dinner
so delicate, you will think you
are eating music." For me,
whole again in every movement
he makes, I imagine Heraclitus
as song. We sing him: step
into the river over wagging fish, over
moving ice, over time so short, it is long.

Vladimir

He is so golden I worry that doubting
Israelites may claim him for worship, and
Moses smash him for his idol glow. He
cannot be distinguished from the burnished
wheat he stands naked amidst behind
my dreaming closed eye. When he moves,
his shoulders light the way, and moony
calves trail after their yellow pillar of salt
to lick him clean of gilding. He is tall
as the Russian sunflowers in open day.

"Move closer," he says. "Move closer to me,"
and beside him I am so subtle I disappear,
white egg compelled back into bird.
"I heard your heart beating," he says, and each
place he touches me grows a shining word.

Vladimir in the Hospital

When the midnight ward is silent,
I come to your hospital bed; run
my hand along the round-edged, blue
tubing that leads to the catheter
piping, pierced in you. Where I touch
is not new, nor the flutter of your
eyelids that welcomes my warm
intrusion. Why I touch you is new.
The cold silver of Kit's ring that rolls
a wheel of cloud up your thigh
across your chest maps you: we are
a million meters west of Moscow,
and the lapis onion-domes grow dim.
Even drugged, your breath quickens and
your eyes nearly open. Your golden skin,
my Eastern riches. Dreaming medicine
in the stealth of my hand, Jerusalem passes over
head—your dark nipples harden. Be well. Triple
God, my own love, enthrall me with this
waiting hell. I touch you to be well.

The End of Chestertown

You want this to be a joyous poem,
tiring sometimes as you do, of my memories.
It is a hazard of loving someone older.
We go places, alone, you have not been.
They seem so separate from us, now. Truth,
they are simply separate. Try—and I do try—
I cannot make sense of who I was:
man of framed picture on your desk, fat
unhappy boy in Cherokee headdress.

Chestertown, my secret gem of widow's
walks, Nike silos, and teenage beach
has aged into nothing but flat, 2-lane
highway, astride white clapboard and
Flemish brick. Doll shows occupy
the feed store, and the dingy bar where
Mark and I bought dope from a sexy,
tattooed farm boy, is now the historic bed
and breakfast where you and I stay.

I know this is the end of Chestertown;
my separation from it can fill the rest
of my life, or be joyous with spectral
visits. How is there an end to anything?
You swear we will not: your faith is
loud as honking pond geese. Midnight,
by the river, "There you are," and you are
pointing high above us, into the vast and
ordered stars. "Was I missing?" You shake
your head at me, my stubborn distance. You
are sure as the town square bell. I love you
forever, with hell still fresh in my mind:
where you touch me, always with care,

is my reflex point of second contact.
You think if you see me do it, it is
compulsion, a physical tie of need to reassurance.
It is not that: I automatically check to see
if I am bleeding, if my lip is thick, my jaw stiff or sore.
A genuflecting puppet show. I am keeping score.

Chestertown ends on a freak, warm day
in January, Chinese New Year, Year of the Dog.
Balmy as LA, hog pens are flower fields,
and the tulip trees you love are fat and hanging;
thirst is lust in freed compulsion: make spring
now; melt snow; hatchlings confuse the river
in crossing lines, and fish go belly up
from warm boredom.

Your cologne, fresh as Christmas, is
still on my shirt. You touch me, even
though I am silent, even with my faith
still new and forearmed for pain. Chestertown
ends in vanity and mistake, like their
tea tax revolt that never took place,
each year reenacted with colonial dress,
wigs and war-painted faces. They commemorate
no history, but create history by believing
time will turn back, wait, and somehow
disengage the state of fact. The end is conscious act.

There is no reach the world won't make.
For I remember a desolate moon, before the plunder
of astronauts, when its cracked, blue light made every
mark on my skin black.

Far across the circumference of me,
your fine square face invites me to joy:

"Come, Captain. The widows that stalked these house peaks have seen a great light: the ships they narrowed for have docked at their doors. Stop pacing; come dance with me, now, on the jubilant shore."
I am yours. It ends. I love you.
Love it all, and love it more.

Shelter

*"When all of this around us falls over, I'll tell you
what we're going to do: You will shelter me, my
love, and I will shelter you."*
--Ray Lamontagne

Coming to terms with shelter
is how we find safety. It
is not the easy commerce
of lodge, dislodge. Instead,
we circle compulsively round
a bed, but this is not a thing
of sleep; untransported, we
cannot lie down. We listen:
twisted Juliet, fatuous Romeo,
confused by birdsong they both
know; compliant guilt, or a wish
to be dead and gone.
                              Refuge is
what we die for, and we cry
ourselves to sleep still standing.
We do not move: a lover will
find us, wake us with a kiss
to dream endless dreams
of his kissing. How stupid
must we be to find
the hermit's sensual ecstasy?
We love one another
and die. He will kiss
someone else to awaken;
so might I. But drilled
to the center of our eye,
behind the iris changing color,
blistered in the palm of the

ever-stroking hand is knowing:
lonely love will vanish; autumn
chills the floor—a yellow bedroom—
a door opens to reveal
you are saved only to save
another. You love this way
only once. White you saw as white,
indigo now. Evening settles,
and he is in your arms right now.
Not tomorrow—he was not there
earlier in the day. Hold him
in the refuge you endure. Nothing
can hurt you. Tonight you are
shelter and sheltered, and sure.

Dangerous

"Love me little, love me long."
-- Christopher Marlowe, "The Jew of Malta,"

When all the world dissolves
where will you look for shelter?
Suddenly, everyone is purified,
and, by divide, all else is hell.
Are we in danger that way?
You say, "This is feeling dangerous,"
and I am sure you are right.
But through every black night
I am looking for the dangerous light
that leads me. I have been
in hell before, wingless, drowning
in honey, stingless, knowing
what was sweet would be, finally,
wasp curling fire around me: end blindly,
blankly in the way a lonely man lives.
I do live that way.
                    Living on nothing can
also make the heart full, but darkness
is best, if, at center of the hollow swell
I find still a little of what now is shell.
The thought, memory of it—what could be
or was, glimmers. But dark must be dark
and through it we feel our way.

When is the day we fold away
all we have been? When
is the day, eyeless, without love or peace
of heart, we are living on what has broken
in two? Such a simple sum: There is no one.
We are dangerous. What we do, feel,

lose, covet, invest, steal, and long
for are so dangerous we cannot say
out loud the nature that invents it. If
I lost you, Edward in all his sorrow—
quartered, dead, at the center of love—
could not engender this stark terror
I have not knowing what I have,
not knowing what would have left me.

In Edward's sky, that wedge of storks he saw,
though flying, stood still—like
the image of Gaveston in his heart, unscathed
by time—the dangerous flight, pure arc
of us across that melting sky, is in my eye,
pupil-center, iris the color of you.
You, the danger, you the peace, you the god of true
burning wisdom, which comes only from two.

Change, Again

From here on I leave happiness to you.
I knew the moment you said it,
love would not be enough. I will
never explain it: love comes late,
no matter how it aches to appear.
I will wear happiness now and stare
ahead. Whatever comes is fair.
In time, nothing will surprise me:
your final lesson learned, books
closed with a day's-end thud.
Teaching one's self is like stopping blood
flow: it is happy to be stopped, but
it waits to explode when bandage tears. Soon
it is all over the room.

The End of the Telegraph

For Marguerite Ryder-Large

Is something you mention in the top
deck of a transit bus in London,
and it comes up again, later in our
room, as we talked about Jane Austen.
I couldn't explain why it made me cry,
why the winnowing world, in opposition
to an exploding majesty, flits like
a fly, expands its wings, dies.
"Your Russian heart," you say, smile,
pure warmth, at my tears. I
remember telegrams, the lightning
words that traveled in clicks and
knocks. My God. So much meaning
in whirling clock hands, seconds,
the beating heart for the first time
coded in standard tick tock
of hate, love, horror: stars
in the first imprint of radiant deviation.
Life could ride with us.

We live beside ourselves, the great
human divide forever parallel. Then,
it is over, and we are taught exactly
what hath God wrought. He
is prickly and excited that we measure
him now. No Russian heart,
no longing for what has passed.
We are our own comfort. Last week
gone to what we write. It is all
afternoon light through the filtering
trees, a staging of greatness, and

a small room, closed to the decoding
of time, of reenacted joy, rage:
POLAND HAS FALLEN; PARIS STILL HERE.
DAD: HE WAS BORN AUGUST 5TH.
KIT, MEET ME AT UNION STATION,
I AM COMING HOME.

Dressing for the Broken Life

My friend Stiles made lists of what
he wore to funerals: black was not it.
The patterns of his ties, full or half
Windsor knots, and the cufflinks—my God—
it filled his little Venetian leather notebook.

So many friends died, my book
has only space for their names:
couples decamping to single entries
or disappearing. Each becomes a
curriculum, a solitary vigor,
a complete abstraction of handwriting.

Widows in groups at my mother's
holiday party favored sweaters,
heavy knits of red, green, and white; some
with tiny silver bells, large diamond
stars, emerald Christmas tree pins
to set off their fading eyes.

Stiles was right; full details of deep
sadness, hints for living out our broken
lives. This morning I looked for your
white socks and remembered
Catherine Sloper's ruby buttons—
the ones she bought for Morris while
she still loved him and waited for her
father to soften to their union. Buttons
were all Morris ever got. Standing
like an idiot at my mirror, I recalled
that was Henry James's fiction. Catherine
seemed a friend; I forgot.
Like Clarinda in her mother's mink, me

in my father's suede wedding shoes,
I wear most of you: half of me,
the mortal tatters obligingly fit,
from bone trees, skeletal closets.

You are not to be seen beneath
appearances that tell of you.
The magic river in Farmington—
Stevens knew it—is what you wear,
the sea you put on. How do I approximate
in tie, trouser, half of that? Looking down
I see my mother's knuckled hands,
her purple, stinging, hypodermic needle
blooms. We lose it all and wear it like a crown,
beauty in half of everything. Now, the stillness
sits in fugitive closets to honor approaching fit.
Someday, your long, artist's hands
will wear your grandfather's
black onyx wedding band.

Kit Teaches Richard Wilbur

He is prepared to lead them on a journey
out of themselves completely. He is armed,
a small arsenal--the pathetic fallacy,
seasons of the year, a rime scheme,
and a simple belief that what he says
will matter. Does it matter? The
beautiful changes are with us:
the half-eaten bowl of cereal sogs
with swelling milk, a boy in front
adjusts his glasses to make
the words fix to meaning on the page.
They move through the poem, a troop
of eye-feet; they turn about, making
a trail. Will he get back home
after so long out? Is he sure?
Lizard makes the leaf leafier, obscure:
we are all deeper than the depth
we sound. Kit's eyes glance down
to see: what he reads is sweet decay.
It leads back to his heart. He changes
as he talks. Spring lesson for a hybrid day.
Leaving them, he is called and starts to follow
his own life, so new; he is filling
in himself, what was hollow. He will
say it better, alone, or to me.
The beautiful changes in the rarity
of everyday—called to the things
of this world, he gives them up
to the fecund memory of eight months'
love, to loud women drinking in the alley
behind his house, to the sudden recognition
of how he watches. And change makes
him beautiful and eager to rise up,

answer for himself, the way he is,
the first time: he is the prize, all
that matters is the small devise we
have become. Deep in the blue pool
he teaches from, conscious at once
of the rule metaphor makes, even of him.
He is the thing about the poem: he is speaker,
the mutating season, reason, that
lengthening reach above the poem.
He says find me here, you who are here,
you who will come. I will love you,
and love you, and love you, and love you:
You who stay; you who come.

The Genius of Love

I am fragile. Remember they will all
be fragile. With you, smooth as twined
velvet, it may not be enough.
Think of your "Keats" photograph of me,
taken at your age. We do not change,
and if you look closely in my photo's
distant eye, some rage reveals that
knowledge. Work with that:
hold his face, as you didn't do mine,
in your long hands; allow your forehead
to rest against his: it is the warmest
touch and says, "All you think
is safe with me." His heart follows.

Never let him drift at sea. Think
always of Penelope, faithful in vacancy.
She did as I will do: stitch backward.
Hers is a love that grows in memory.
Faint at first, a tapestry of flowers,
then wind and ocean, her loom
pounds like thunder in reverse
all night. She waits; he comes.
But I teach a new design:
no line leads to figure; it
is a disappearing man she loves, creates.

Love him as you loved me, but with more
tactile reality all around. Car keys
placed in the same place: they are the light
in the hall. It is a light you
learned from me, but filled with what
you will still be tomorrow, stars
that get in each other's way.

Endless things framed not by departure
or return, but how you learn to hold
the endless in your hand, to know
fading image in your mirror—
the one we hung—reflects a new face,
the one you love and returns everyday.

Prayer for Kit at Windsor Locks

Perhaps I speak for you in lower frequencies now,
or say nothing, and you hear me. As the teaching
grows dumb, you finally learn me. Your own mystery
trumpets at you: you imagine without me a bed
at the top of Heaven, so new, you smell
wood, fragrant, cut in two and made for you.

    It is talk like prayer, modulated so
that listening draws us closer: sound we
must hear. Compassion in the air—scent
of orthodox candles a million bees give to God
to burn for us.

    And if you speak softly, love so musical in your voice,
he will learn you. I become you. Lead him inward 'til he
finds you, my man of square countenance and stubborn
hair. In your bridal bower wear the red blood of me—on
his chest, in my sun-worn eyes so weary with care,
you lie in his arms, on his pillow finally there.

    That I share with you this longing,
our impossible pairing of twin desires, a soft
word, the wrapping stare of loneliness, the final care
I give, bears you up, still so dearly loved, silently,
into soft, delphinium, star-gazer, narcissus-scented air.

Aubade

Frightened as Hitler must have been,
to wake that morning and know he
was so past evil, watching a rat crawl
out of his ass. Too many days start
like this, past the ceiling caving in, bed
flattened by the plaster lattice, your
face wider than the overhead
forced into your mouth.
                                    South of here
flamingos sweep pink, their black tips
of beak dapple, dull spots of retina
detachment in the blue-eyed sky.
Why go back? Numb daylight is ahead
and you are free to be blank forever.
This is not death, suicide drama. It is
the ribbon you, pale strip, trauma living
on the edge of the wooden box you build—
house, scaffold, dome, your majestical
roof fretted with crayon fire: base lyric
of base desire, a chance to feel for
the webbing that holds the choir of leaking
love in check. Necks innocently snapped
on the newly polished stairs. You are
staring back from a gray TV screen.
Wake up, my love. Wake up scared.

When Kit Listens

"As for our harps, we hanged them up upon trees."
-- Psalms 137:2

Loving you is so quiet now.
Beneath the broken harness, unbridled
from all we pulled, movement has slowed,
and something golden, your head turning
to hear, brought me rest when I feared
there was none. Centered to the cut
of feeling, I am sleeping. All allowed
within us, the single eye of sun. Endless
as aether, the drug beneath our flying
skin is time. I think, "This is how
it feels, the clock set back I am wound in."
I dream Modigliani's dream: upright,
tall as God's thigh. Soft as April's petal snow—
finally, our sound reverses time.
Day after day, our harps
hung upon willows, sweep our faces
clean of pain, back from fragile Job,
aching to ecstasy and the subtly spinning globe.

Leaning on Icarus

For Melissa Sherrill

My sister tells you I crave chaos.
Rather, I believe, I have made
a home for it in all I do.
Sara's class of children, special
in their funneled sight, see
a baby's coffin, white and
single as a first lost tooth, that
slept on, becomes a silver dollar
at the end of night. Your
chaotic sorrow that visits
in lonely blight and follows
you, a hummingbird: pool
of dark nectar, bright ribs
from which you build
a legless night to run fast
and eyeless far above me.
What form—the waiting boyfriend,
the vengeful father—arrival, departure,
the sudden rapture of disjointed anger
that dissipates into lonely love—what
we know. Chaos in the square hearts
we pace away in even measure,
every room a forge to make ourselves,
every room a passage to the start of day.

Jonestown's Kool-Aid suicide, Beckett's
whining clowns: I am chaos, and
you love me. Grasp for wings
how Icarus taught me: higher
to drop, plummeting to myth,
to Bruegel, to Auden to drown
to live again; down, to matter to drown.

The Complexities of Delray Beach

For David Parker

The ocean lies there with a whine
that hums all night long: high tension
wires coiled in monotonous sound circles,
flat to the shore. Men disappear there
into email caves; the ethernet vacuum
sucks their beauty into lost silver rings
in the sand, into solitary canvas shoe,
green as a hermit crab; or into other
men's mouths, as words spoken
backwards, garbled, wholly eaten.
Nothing stares or blinks. Sometimes
at night, the ghost of a rippled stomach,
buffalo shoulders, passes through you
while you stand outside the motel
of failed assignation to smoke. You
are speechless for seconds, like a tiny
stroke has tickled one side of your face.
The cigarette falls in graceless, dead-drop
dive. Its coal is cold before
it hits ground, and you are old.

Hero and Leander

For Stephen Daniel Ciesielski

Only fire moves like this, hoping
in time to expire by its own immolation.
Bordered by cinder outline, I see
the wires that held your stars in place.
I am latitude, the flat sea. Staying still,
all things will float to me, and the line
you chart from me is a perfidy so
close to dance, fish confuse it for flame.

There is no name for this: whale bones
sink like a storm of worms, fall deeper
into wet death. No breath left, the bubble
cipher trapped forever where you are.
It is hard, hearing fire above, teeth
chewing water below. Like Hero
and Leander, at once silly and profound:
one whom fire burnt, one whom water drowned.

Kit's Scorched-Earth Policy

He was not alive when the Joint Chiefs
devised the scorched-earth policy for
North Vietnam: those half-eaten
children, clothes burned off, hopping
on one leg, by fallow rice paddies.
But some Pulitzer war photo hung
for him, accessible, and converted
into housing for the way he said
goodbye. 24 hours since, and I am
one-armed, skinned where
his eyes touched my face. I
will make sense of this: He always
gave me what I wanted. From
the whitest snow to the tightest
poem, forest of words cut down
to simple, direct meaning. Napalm
over everything. All I collected as
the blessing after fall was really
all or nothing. I got nothing
as a last lesson. Tall things, short
nubs of shrieking love
blown away. Prints in ash
all over my apartment. And
Kit becomes spectral against
the yellow dining-room walls.
Was he here, extinguished, or his
form a vitreous floater?
It kills me: I believe I
hear him cry. Ears gone,
lids a crackled halo over burned-blind eyes.

Jonathan's Ghost

*"The years are long and full of sharp, wearing days that wear
out what we are and what we have been and change us into
people we do not know, living among strangers. Hear this,
lest you and I who love should wake some morning strangers
and enemies in an alien world far off."*
  -- Maxwell Anderson "Elizabeth, the Queen"

I don't remember if I loved him. But a bone lust
of feeling sweeps through me when I think of David.
It was not as I expected: in death I did not find him
again. He promised so much to me in those still nights
of reverie, wolves howling at the purple moon that hung
like a whore's spangle above Gilead. Who knows what
he really said. We were lost in each other, lives entangled
then. I know he lied to me over and over, sharp pin gleam
in the mountain snow where we lay. He will say I made
him lie to comfort me; fear was all around. It must be so.
I didn't care when what he told me was said so close to my
ear, my face grew chilled as the warm moisture of his
whispered breath evaporated in the night's thin, dry air.

I am night, now, everywhere, and the lies he told cover
me, fish scales. I swim, flipping in obliterated seas made
desert by his hopeful, dishonest care. Love, friendship—too
rare to make my home; filtered through death they are a two-
headed snake, a crawling bird, a rock that sings, "Take me,
take me, lest I wake to find the world a blank madness, hard
and nothing." We were nothing. Help me find him. Make
me an angel that flies from here. Wings made of harp notes
that he played long ago.
Give me one song that I might hold to. To believe that he
loved me is a hard way to go.

Disappear

I never believed you could do this: make me disappear.
But you threw away the pictures, after dinner at L'etranger,
us on the sofa when you laid your head on my shoulder
and said, "Let's stay here in London forever." After you
held the camera above us to snap that fragile
moment in time, the dreary rain in the Notting Hill
night, the smell of burnt candles' extinguished light,
and the rare, real memento mori posed on the chair
beside us; I found the photo you'd slipped
from the packet crammed to the side of the
wastepaper basket in our room.
                              Don't you know?
Magic will reverse: everything diminished grows
large again. That tiny moment in your frightened
eyes will swell to billboard size; how you hate me
now will vitalize into pain too big to throw away,
move aside, or ever make disappear. Nothing
disposed, image upon image overexposed
in the terrible camera you are. Now
you are who you said you would never
become. I ask myself how long I knew
you would finally be the winking pearl
of cruelty clamped in my heart. I disappear,
and you develop, full, aching color, in the dark.

That Old Picture of Me

The one you loved so much, laughed at,
the one you sat on the desk where you
wrote, is gone now, isn't it? I know
you swallowed hard when you threw
it away. That was the man you wrote
to; that was the man you thought
about, saw in your mind's eye as
you left my house each night. The balding
me, the broken one you tried to fix,
kept lumbering forward in your mix of poetry,
daydream, and loss. I am disgraced now,
years older. The fortune in my eyes reads
death and displacement. All men's eyes
can be read: desiring another's art,
his scope of feeling, what you read
in me. In that picture, even 25 years
before you appeared, my eyes were
fixed on you. As though I'd know
you when you came, bootless, sad,
quivering to fly, a revving engine
of bright lark song and midnight.
The picture you remember: how I am
at this end, scorn and stifled wonder.
Change your state with nothing. Beneath
the surface, the glossy face, is a closet
of worn shoes, lost keys on the floor,
a rainbow of shirts you cannot
use and never wore.

My Sexy Cowboy Calendar

Their guns, outlined in jeans,
are always cocked. No art here,
we are meant to imagine ourselves—
mouths, fists, butts—as their holsters.
None has the chewed-up look John Ford
perfected; instead, they are the pink-nippled,
pumped chest of Monty Clift in Levi Strauss
drag.
       They are unbidden as all dreams: veil
eyed pokes with dicks too big to ever sit
a horse. What is waking? Next year
they may be Vikings, bear fur hardly
covering their vortex of thigh; or in 2008,
rapacious pirates whose single shot pistols
tent their pantaloons. I wish to wake
to monthly photos of the doctor down
the block, his bald head gleaming
above his tank-topped sides, the tumescent
swelling that rides his waistband he knows
I observe as he walks his dogs
by me each day, with downcast eyes.

Saved

"...in absence work out your own
salvation with fear and trembling."
*   -- Philippians 2:12*

What is the use of talking? It is
a worrisome cough, a hacking
heard through the neighbors' wall,
indistinct, but menacing. When
we stopped talking, I listened
every night for other signals: light
that would carry music, or, from
far away, the safe rhythmic noise
of your fingers clicking on the letters
of your keyboard; that voiceless voice
of drawn words, meaning something.
There is no end of talking in the dark.

Absence is a language spoken to itself:
utterance untransfigured; no pattern,
no random shooting star to change,
to augur what we are. There is an end
to things in the heart. A place where
feral children are yoked to dull domesticity,
their jangling knees stilled to drugged love
and complicity with the thud, thud, thud
of empty heart. We do not go on. We
are the men of whom St. Paul said
God is in their bellies. Feed us
on strangers whose kindness is
inadvertent, whose broken lives
mount, unplanned, to big blue Wyoming
skies. Where cowboys fuck us with
ragged sighs of loss and their spotted

calves cry out, a mystery chorus
of unfathomed passion, disconsolate desire.
You will think we have been visited by fire;
but we know, have always known
what was coming: Disbelief saved me.
You were saved, lying about what you
believed. Love is measured by stippling
on our skin. Now, work with bruise,
absence, fear and trembling.

Carnival

For Sydney Gingrow

In the South, we waited for them:
a ritual of summer heat, sticking
to the seats of the Tilt-a-Whirl.
For 10 cents, once, my father pitched
a baseball through the sawed-out
bottom of a half bushel basket—four
times straight—and won me a prize.
I chose a stuffed tiger, whose popsicle
orange and black stripes made me tingle,
the whole world dancing there.

I lived in my father's eye then; what
he saw became my edgy innocence.
My choice embarrassed him. It was
a bedroom toy for lounging flat
to stare at tacked up cut outs
of Fabian. Not the BBgun he pointed
at. I was five, old enough to understand
why he walked so far ahead of me. Lost,
back in the squalid color, I lingered by
the sleek, wet boy with massive,
pork-fed biceps and read his tattoo
swelling there: "Joy," it said. I was done
at five. We are not just fools, we are mighty ones.

Blue Shirt

For Clarinda Harriss

Sight is taught. Perception
builds upon some brief abstraction
of light and eventually we come near
to visualizing "bombs bursting in air."
Poets delight in how mere light confounds
the untrained senses.
                       For instance,
I was astounded to look at you and
see you red as raw meat: a steak
astride the earth on flat feet. All that
time, your sweet colors belonged in
Butcher Street.

Perfectly Untied

For Bill Hazlehurst

The television allowed me to see
snakes fucking—I draw the line
at attributing love to reptiles, despite
the coral, yellow, and black that
throb away like rainbow crankshafts
in dizzying motion. This piece of natural
pornography held me there, a hypno-
humming bird, until their serpent knot
was gratified, and they perfectly untied.
Bright ends of a V, they were diverging
lines of decanted wine. Like all love—
I said it anyway—they inched away.

The Rest of My Life

Clarinda says a man she knows
earned his beautiful body. Roses
earn red; it is blood by the inch
to burst green buds and color them,
wantonly. Adam's curse: I know,
I know, and I have labored to be
beautiful but failed. Past mid point,
in mid light, and senseless
without gorgeous flesh, wet,
shiny beside me. The rest of my life—
this hummingbird heart that rattles
in purple fusion inside skeletal cage—
with my oh so serious Russian, we
carve out the life we'll lead.
He is the beauty I earned, worn
scarlet, all subsidy and peevish
brilliance. Gone, then gotten.
This is what I've learned.

Chatterton

The lilac-trousered boy lies dead
on his grimy bed. Window propped
for fetid air, he stinks where bladder
failed, and his red curls are dampened
copper on the white, white neck.
        His milky
eye rolled loose from sight wetly stares
at nothing. Lying art could not break his
fall; he hurls outward to posterity, the symbol
of ravaged truth in poetry. No ghostly father
calls him home, his sexual pose in death
a tentative stop on the way to purgation,
to myth, and permanent arousal.

Shoes

My sister wanted red patent leather ones,
"Like Dorothy," she begged. That was
the day I saw the man, a hunchback,
wearing shoes like Frankenstein; they seemed
so big, I stared until my mother pulled me
away from watching how he lifted each foot
and slammed it down so bitterly slow.

The Holocaust Museum with a pile
of them from Nazi kills: school girl
brogans, lace less little raisins dried
to paper. And the shoes that rained
down in burning, bloody torrents from
exploding planes, collapsing towers
on the ash covered world at Ground Zero.

Shoes chosen, fitted and compelled forward
on feet that danced, tripped, kicked, or ran
in free fall of radiant expectation, cobbled
by elves or factory blades; shoes of Luftwaffe
pilots, porn stars, priests, and you.
Line them up in color order under hanging suits,
black, cordovan, ox blood, leather soft as vellum.
Worn in the night glow of stars above our lost Jerusalem.

The Failure of Architecture

Falling Water is falling. Daily
it pops and gapes, an unzipped
fly on some old man. The alarm
goes out to Pittsburgh, New York, Seattle,
wherever the ashen faces of architects
bemoan themselves of punctured landscape.
How do they answer such decline? Circle,
line is all they have to heal the cut
of beauty, and
                          ripe plums are falling,
vacuous, delicious, a thousand mites
crushed under deep, round perfection.
The alarm goes out to anthills, silk cocoons,
and wasps' nests. They cannot mourn,
untouched by upward vanity. Purity
of falling in the fallen thing. They
call on us: give us sting. The blotted
fruit rings out the sweetness of failure
and ultimate conclusion of wet, sticky wing.

Lilies Burning

Greenmount Cemetery caught fire today. Through green
smoke I could barely make out the tinseled Gothic spire
of its chapel mausoleum. 22 fire engines, red as gladiola,
lined up like a spine under vivid x-ray. Crowds of us
walked three blocks to see it burn: John Wilkes Booth,
Betsy Bonaparte, and the empty, rose-shaped plots
of the Duke and Duchess of Windsor. Willow tendrils
curled back like fiddle fern, and the black Norwegian rats
were a crowd of crouching syncopation across the caustic
ground. Finally, the day lilies were burning, their purple,
orange, white, and pink heads bursting like stained glass
in morbid, heat shadow.
                    Tomorrow in the gray, dead jungle,
blackened monuments will steal small glints of sunlight
but remain arranged, silent. The dead are cool while Hell
blazes, and the lilies pump sweet dew from flattened stems.
The cemetery cleans itself, a Burmese cat, with sanguine
piety; in its heart, the moldy stealth of ravaged, stagnant beauty.

The Hay-Adams Hotel

When I was with you, I loved the moon,
its fellowship with night, the square touch of it;
we lived so sure sharp edge awaited us.
When we fell, pain everywhere, secure
in its right to devastate, I got up
from bed in the moon-lit room, dressed
in my suit and paisley tie, and left that place forever
while you slept, your sing-song snore
like mosquitoes in the light,
your tiny, rhythmic sighs so far behind.

Exile's Letter

I want you to hurt: every
knife-thought, every memory plunged
in you. I am in a place where
words are blooms, too difficult and beautiful
to be picked. I am still as a stick.

This is not waiting. Not Grant in Galena
trembling for war nor shiftless St. Paul all
alone in Damascus, counting down to light.

Here the scope of my rifle meets my green
rind of eye. Loss is mystical, a target
spinning round the heart's circumference.

The world lives for panic now, absolves
itself in Twin Tower vigilance, bent
steel vengeance. Self-preservation
is Ground Zero, the mystical no tomorrow.

So sinks the day-star in ocean bed. Look
homeward, angel, and meet the brutal
ending with standard gulp. The hungry
sheep look up and are not fed; they bleat,
"This is a starving place." It is: thin planets
and the Milky Way a mist of razorblades
slicing the day into shards of ever-tinkling
ice cube sky.

You cannot write me here. Nothing
is delivered. If I ever move, it is the
hunchback's posture. I swing
between the cantilevered monuments,
the distaff structures of your comet face.

I am at home here, dressed for dates
with shape-shifters—easy fucks; and
I lie at night by Stephen's broken body;
he permeates your dissemblance
like it was a tease. At last, I immerse,
am purified and raised on high to stink.
Well, honestly, Kit, what did you think?

Finding Atlantis

Atlantis was never hidden, never below
the ocean where Thracian, jeweled laser
guns dispatched B-52s and Soviet MIGs
to molecular dust. The Palace at Knossos
stood in spectacular ruin, always. Children
played in Minos's throne room, hid from each
other behind the gypsum-faced blocks.
Further down, lovers worked their bodies
into vibrant form, skin rippled with an ancient
light, one that prehistoric engineers planned
for, directed. So the mystery that Plato started
was not mysterious at all. Slumber is us, tall
as soldiers coming home, dreaming of red victimhood.
Living with every answer is twisted recompense
for slavery every day. I am in a dark wood,
unmysterious, where loud trees strike thudding
notes upon their own splitting bark. I will learn:
discovery is everywhere, and deceit, another need;
love, pooling urine on the floor from my aging Labrador.
Give all, dog all, to be diminished, but returned.

Distance and the Dead

"The distance that the dead have gone
Does not at first appear--
Their coming back seems possible
For many an ardent year."
    -- Emily Dickinson

For Jane Siegel

They do come back, in the anonymity of airports,
in the standard Hilton room. Dante was right:
there is no transcendence, for death is only personal.
I have known it on the midnight concourse, gate 47 E,
as I float, descend into food-court mall, the ratcheted
shops of suburban Thanatopia. No city seems remote:
the ones you thought dead have migrated with you
to populate every street corner with themselves. Stephan's
musky scent cheats the breeze and stops you, stunned,
by the Starbucks in Northampton. Daniel's hand
is on the apple you touch in Produce at the Whole Foods
Market, his skin so real, you jerk your arm away, electrocuted
by a current of sensuality that has no stem or vine.
The clouded petals of Robin Harriss's boutonniere have dropped
on the tops of your scuffed shoes, and the shock of white,
flaming in Benita's hair, becomes a silence too vivid to bear.

I believe these things are real; not the muck of pale brains
that wander, séance-silly, through spectral life. The dead
remain in us, see us in our vacancies. They arrive
in thin whistles from pine tree knots, measure distance
like the seizure of a migraine, are witness
to our deepest, settling surrenders.

Lovely and afraid, marked for plunder, white-eyed,

skittish as a summer moon, we are their hands,
weight, scent, their obdurate redundancy. They travel
in the stark admission of all we take away, daily:
coat sleeve, hairbrush, Tylenol, dream. They
are whom we make. We are their mistakes.

The World Is Lit by Lightning, Kit, and So, Goodbye

"Methought I saw my late espoused Saint
brought to me like Alcestis from the grave."
*   -- John Milton, Sonnet XXIII*

I will die, a figment flying through your dream,
your veiled and fancied sight, to sonar beacon.
A bat aimed at finely tuned, sleepy sound, your sorrow
pitch. What did we miss in that night room which may
give way to full sight in Heaven? I wait until then,
mosquito feeder, the night fever you shiver from: red,
all in red the Temple tears itself in two; you feel for
fluttering life up under the dark body, coal webbing,
in shaking lunar fit. Then blood: the sunrise is a blood
corona. It is everywhere. All, all over.

Kit's Prayer for Me

Forgive him for throwing me away;
for choosing nothing in a field of splendor
when what I offered was every day
unplundered, straitened heart.
That love is not art, wed
to those photographs of lost men
above his bed. Show him
and prove: I was his genius of love.

Move him when he is paralyzed.
Carry him away on skating rivers,
ice the depth of Farmington, white
snow his only bed of dreaming hope.
Keep music in his angry, cracking
throat to sing my name when ships
are sinking, John Donne preaching
his tolling bells, Auden digging stars
from carry-out cartons in East Village
trash. Make him last in me without me.
Teach him not to lie: symmetry
is fleeting, but the fearful sleep
untouched, advent or absence,
buried in skull reflection. Let
me remember and forgive him,
neither supplicant nor savior, for
what he meant to give.

Let him live—a crow's cry, monkey
screech, a cello note made sleek
in my memories of him. Rats sleep
docile in his pockets; worms fan out,
a crown around his head. Show, by showing
prayer is valid, that you have trained

with patient divinity, all moments to fall,
just and dazzling, a spring snow squall
on him. Then, he who has never known
happiness, and I, with all happiness
to give, will live again in each other.
Meeting by a car on the dirt road to Gidding,
or on a night train from Hoboken; in
a cyclone of birch trees; in the pale glow
from a lit window above us on a street
in Kensington when the shade goes up
so we might know forgiveness and forgiveness:
a battered light Henry James might show
the unnamed man in sensuous
retreat from love's haunted echo.

Help me to forgive his greed of me.
Prepare his harvest: speed the plow.
Give him rest from his labor of loving me.
Rest as he wanted: he has no one again.
But let him find rest.
                         May he not feel alone
without me. Bend the world to fit his heart.
Find him, love him through the crooked
ways of loss. Lift him, raise him softly
over empty time. In his speechless
days of yearning, teach him, as he waits
for me, free of me, how to love again,
how to praise. Under you, God
of random shattering wonder, I
pray inside your thunder and forgetfulness:
our love is a fiery wreckage growing dim,
melting shirt buttons, mateless cufflinks,
broken glasses, aging skin. Remember it all
and forgive what I did; redeem what I
gave, what I lost in him.